D1712064

I Feel Mad! Tips for Kids on Managing Angry Feelings

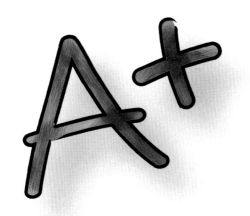

YOU ARE AWESOME!

In fact, every kid that we know or have ever met is awesome.

Some kids have a little extra challenge with managing angry feelings in a safe manner. This may be true for you.

This workbook includes ideas and strategies you can try to make things work better for you and to help you manage those angry feelings, which can be scary or get you into trouble at home or at school.

WHAT YOU WILL NEED:

 Your brain ready to brainstorm!

 A pencil to write down ideas.

 A healthy snack is always nice!

WE HAVE A QUESTION FOR YOU.
Do you think that being *MAD* is *BAD*?

GUESS WHAT?

Being mad is not bad at all. It's just another feeling, such as being happy or being excited.

It's what you do when you are mad that might cause problems or get you into trouble.

MAD is usually the second emotion you feel. Maybe you first feel

- **Disappointed** because you can't have what you want.

- **Frustrated** because you didn't expect a change in plans.

- **Resentful** because your brother or sister is being bossy.

- **Lonely** because no one is listening to you.

- **Helpless** because school is really hard.

- **Sad** because your feelings are hurt.

- **Ashamed** or **embarrassed** about something that happened.

When anger starts with one of those first emotions, that angry feeling can quickly become too hot to handle. Take the temperature of your anger and use our tips before the angry feeling hits the top of the thermometer.

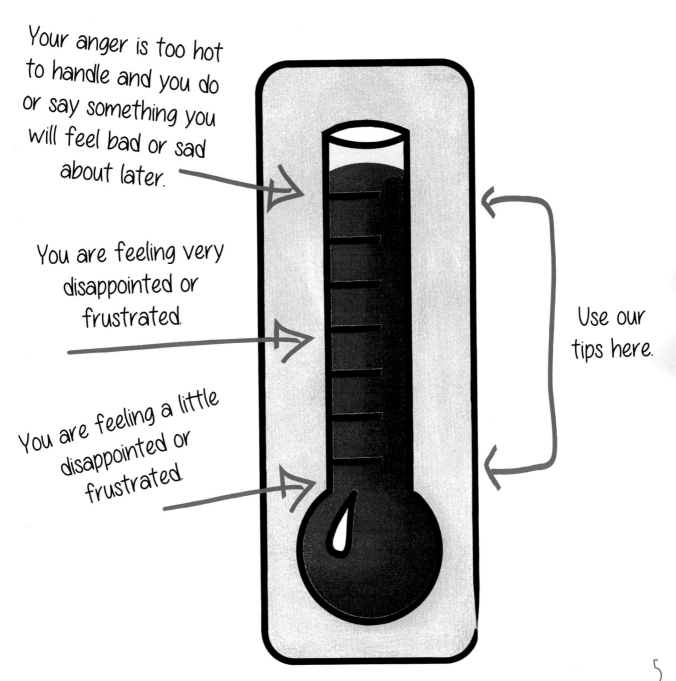

Your anger is too hot to handle and you do or say something you will feel bad or sad about later.

You are feeling very disappointed or frustrated.

You are feeling a little disappointed or frustrated.

Use our tips here.

WHAT MAKES YOU MAD?

people pushing

people make fun of me

people annoy

Someone coming into my room

Trying to do too much/ multitasking

I Feel Mad!: Tips for Kids on Managing Angry Feelings

CAN YOU TELL US WHAT THE RULES ARE?
At School:

✓ Listen to the teacher.

✓ Do your school work neatly and completely.

You might be thinking...

✓ No running in the halls.

✓ Turn your homework in on time.

✓ Keep your hands to yourself.

Or at the Library:

✓ Use a whispering voice.

You might be thinking...

✓ Put books and materials away when you are done with them.

✓ Check out books with a library card.

✓ Return the books on time.

Most kids know what rules are!

I Feel Mad!: Tips for Kids on Managing Angry Feelings

DID ANYONE EVER TELL YOU
THAT THERE ARE RULES ABOUT
BEING MAD, TOO?

YUP ... THERE ARE!

Actually, there is
just **one** important
rule to remember.

And that rule is...

STOP

DO NO HARM!

TO YOURSELF OR OTHERS!

THIS RULE MEANS:

You may not harm anyone else, neither **with your body** nor **with your words.**

What are some examples?

Hitting

Kicking

Pushing

Biting

Pinching

Name calling

Swearing

THIS ALSO MEANS:

You may not harm yourself, neither **with your body** nor **with your words.**
What are some examples?

Holding your breath

Scratching yourself

Banging your head

Pinching your arm

Stomping your feet

Threatening to hurt yourself

Calling yourself names

Bolting or running away

Being unsafe in any way

And

You may not harm or destroy your own or other people's things on purpose.

What are some examples?

Wrecking your brother's or sister's project

Slamming doors

Throwing your game controller

Punching walls

Ripping up your schoolwork or homework

One of the ways you can help yourself to stop and do no harm when you feel angry is to recognize when you are **starting** to feel mad.

Your body will tell you when you are mad.

Everyone feels their anger in their body in a different way.

Think about how _your_ body feels when you are getting angry.

Think about

        ✓ Your head

            ✓ Your arms and hands

        ✓ Your legs and feet

            ✓ Your stomach

        ✓ Your chest

Maybe

            ✓ You sweat

      ✓ You feel like smoke is coming out of your ears

            ✓ Your face gets red and feels hot

      ✓ Your chest hurts

            ✓ Your stomach feels like it's on fire

      ✓ You clench your fists or teeth

Draw or color how your body feels when you are getting angry.

I Feel Mad!: Tips for Kids on Managing Angry Feelings

You have the **power** to make a choice when you start to feel mad.

You can choose to be angry safely, or you can choose to do something that will get you into trouble.

Remember how at the beginning of the workbook we asked you to bring your brain to our chat?

Let's brainstorm some things you **can** do when you are angry.

Here are some safe ideas to try!
(Choose the ones that would work for you.)

Draw a picture of how mad you are and put it in the freezer to cool off.

Stomp on or pop a big piece of bubble wrap.

Blow your anger away with some bubbles.

Maybe Take a break and remove yourself from what or who is making you angry.

And a few more:

maybe

Dig a hole, put your anger in it, and stomp on the dirt.

Write what you are mad about on an egg and throw it outside, *maybe* (with your parent's permission).

Take a nap or eat a snack if you are feeling tired or hungry.

Rip up old magazines or newspapers in the recycle bin.

Find a place to be alone and yell, cry, or hit a pillow.

X Talk to your pet if you have one. A stuffed animal can work, too.

Read a book, *maybe* watch TV, or listen to music.

X Exercise or do a high-energy activity.

Some of those tips might not work at school. If you are at school, you could also try these ideas:

✗ Listen to yourself breathe. If you are really angry, it might sound loud.

✗ 3 + 10 = Take three deep belly breaths and then count to 10.

✗ Press the palms of your hands together.

✗ Imagine a stop sign in your brain to stop yourself from becoming angrier.

21

Here are some more ideas:

Rub your hands on your legs.

Tell people how you feel by using "I" statements (we'll talk about how later in the book).

Find a friend or an adult to talk to, as long as you don't shout at them.

Imagine each part of your body becoming relaxed.

Tell yourself that being mad doesn't solve problems, and then try to solve the problem.

Maybe

Stop an argument by saying you need a break, then walk away.

Maybe

Think of something calm, like floating on a cloud or being on a beach.

Maybe

Maybe

Tell yourself that you are bigger than your anger.

23

Try brainstorming some of your own ideas here:

I Feel Mad!: Tips for Kids on Managing Angry Feelings

Once your anger is under control, you will be able to work on solving the problem or problems that made you mad in the first place.

Most problems are solvable with a little extra brainstorming. Let's practice brainstorming solutions to some common problems together.

The problem: **Your favorite TV show is on at the same time as your brother's or sister's favorite show.**

Possible solutions:

1. Agree to watch your show on odd-numbered days and her show on even-numbered days.

2. Flip a coin to choose which show to watch.

3. Ask whether you can watch your show on another TV.

4. Watch a little bit of each show.

5. Record your show if you have a DVR.

6. Offer to let him or her watch his or her show, but you get to choose the next one.

7. <u>Go do something else</u>

"I Feel FRUSTRATED"

HERE'S ANOTHER ONE!

The problem: Something you were counting on won't happen (for example, you have plans to go to the amusement park, but it's raining).

"I Feel DISAPPOINTED"

Possible solutions:

1. Make a plan B and go to the movies instead.

2. Pick a different date.

3. Invite a friend over to play for the day.

4. Stay flexible, even if you are really disappointed.

5. Go to an indoor amusement place.

6. Tell yourself that, even though it's a big deal to you, it's not an emergency.

7. _____

ONE MORE!

The problem: Your mom tells you to shut off your video game and do your homework.

Possible solutions:

1. Next time, do your homework before you begin to play.

2. Do as she asks without arguing; then maybe you can earn extra time to play.

3. Agree not to play video games on school nights, but set aside game time on weekends.

4. Agree to set a timer for 5 more minutes to transition from the game to your homework.

5. Ask whether you can pause your game while you do your homework so you don't lose your place.

6. Do 15 minutes of homework with a 5 minute game break in between.

7. _____

NOW IT'S YOUR TURN!

Think of a problem that happens to you a lot and then brainstorm solutions.

The problem: _____

_____

_____

Possible solutions:

1. _____
2. _____
3. _____
4. _____
5. _____
6. _____
7. _____
8. _____

I Feel Mad!: Tips for Kids on Managing Angry Feelings

REMEMBER THESE THREE WORDS TO KEEP YOURSELF OUT OF TROUBLE:

1. Talk

Explain your problem. For example, you can say, "I don't like it when _____ and I want it to stop." Use a firm, strong voice without yelling.

2. Walk

Walk away from the situation that is making you mad.

3. Ask

If you don't know how to solve the problem on your own, ask a trusted adult for help. You could say, "I'm frustrated and I need some help to solve a problem."

ARGUMENTS CAN REALLY MAKE PEOPLE ANGRY.

HERE ARE THREE OTHER WORDS TO REMEMBER THAT CAN HELP STOP AN ARGUMENT (think of them as fire prevention):

1. Stop

Stop responding and arguing back.

2. Drop

Drop the subject.

3. Roll

Roll with it by saying something like:

You might be right.

Let's agree to disagree.

Let's work this out when we calm down.

A GOOD QUOTE TO KEEP IN MIND:

" I don't have to attend every argument I'm invited to. "

When you need to tell someone that you are angry, how you feel, or what you need and you want to have them listen to you, try these words (this is called an "I" statement):

I FEEL
Example: I feel angry

WHEN
Example: when someone comes into my room without permission

BECAUSE
Example: because sometimes I like my privacy

AND I WANT, NEED, or WISH:
Example: and I want people to knock first.

Let's practice a few of those "I" statements for some of the strong feelings you might have:

I feel disappointed when _____
because _____ , and I want
(or need or wish) _____ .

I feel frustrated when _____
because _____ , and I want
(or need or wish) _____ .

I feel resentful when _____
because _____ , and I want
(or need or wish) _____ .

Try these! Telling someone how you feel becomes easier with practice.

I feel lonely when _____
because _____ , and I want
(or need or wish) _____ .

I feel helpless when _____
because _____ , and I want
(or need or wish) _____ .

I feel sad when _____
because _____ , and I want
(or need or wish) _____ .

And a few more!

I feel impatient when _____
because _____ , and I want
(or need or wish)_____ .

I feel ashamed when _____
because _____, and I want
(or need or wish) _____.

I feel mad when _____
because _____ , and I want
(or need or wish)_____ .

Your parents or an older family member are great people to ask for help. Sometimes it is really hard to learn to manage your anger without extra support. There are also special adults who are trained to help if you need them.

They can be

school counselors

social workers

social coaches

psychologists

It is OK to ask for help when you feel mad!

I Feel Mad!: Tips for Kids on Managing Angry Feelings

That's it!

Thank you so much for brainstorming with us. We would be happy to hear from you. Send us any questions or comments you have by email and we will be sure to respond you as soon as we can.

We would also love to hear what you thought about these tips and whether they helped you manage your angry feelings in a safe way after you gave them a try.

We are also always interested in new ideas that kids come up with! Your mom, dad, or another adult can help you write us an email at howtomakeandkeepfriends@gmail.com

- Miss Donna & Miss Nadine

About the Authors

Donna Shea and Nadine Briggs are both accomplished social educators. They each facilitate friendship groups at their respective centers in Massachusetts. Both Nadine and Donna are parents of children with special needs.

Donna and Nadine offer consultation services for schools, parent groups, and human-service agencies. They are seasoned public speakers who travel across the country to bring workshops and seminars to schools, conferences, and other venues.

Donna and Nadine are certified in bullying prevention through the Massachusetts Aggression Reduction Center and are creators of the How to Make & Keep Friends Bullying Prevention Initiative that is used to provide classroom training and team-building activities at many schools.

Donna and Nadine would love to hear from you or your child if you have feedback about this book. They are also happy to speak with you about providing programming for children in your local area or just to keep in touch with you about new books and materials.

Email us at howtomakeandkeepfriends@gmail.com

"...this is an impressive, handy resource. It suggests solutions for easily recognizable difficulties, such as aggression or shyness, as well as more subtle ones, such as "not understanding humor" or "rigid thinking."
- Kirkus Review

My son is having a little trouble with a friend- he grabbed your book and started reading sections 3 & 4... I love this. We have the book on the counter - so if anyone needs some support they know right where to find it.
- Lisa

At some point, every child experiences social challenges. Whether your child just needs help with the occasional awkward moment, or is experiencing some really difficult situations, this book comes to the rescue with quick "what-to-do" tips that are easy to learn and can be used right away. Recently, my son invited a friend over, so we reviewed the tips on "How to Be a Good Playdate Host," and the afternoon went great! We have also used the tips on sharing, attending parties, and working together in groups. The tips offer a nice springboard for conversations about an upcoming situation, or to help process situations after they have occurred. I don't think this book will ever make it to a shelf in our house - we keep it handy and refer to it almost every day! This is a *must-have* book for every parent!
- Joan

This is a great book for children, parents, educators, and anyone who works with children! I am a principal aide for grades 3 through 5, and deal with many children from different backgrounds and with different disabilities. This book is a wonderful guide to help children make friends and learn how to get along in social situations.
- Kim

What a great, practical book!!!! Nicely done! I love it. It clearly identifies the social and problem solving skills that so many people take for granted (and that some just really don't know) and puts them into a usable, practical, and simple format that not only teaches, but also reminds us ALL about how we can better get along with each other!! Nicely done!
- Sue

69609418R00027

Made in the USA
Lexington, KY
02 November 2017